Minding My Mind

'Wonuola Akintola

GRATITUDE

All gratitude to The Mind Maker, for equipping and empowering me in this journey, and enriching this mind with other minds.

Contents

ACKNOWLEDGMENTS

To my ever-supportive trio. Your contribution is priceless.
Thank you for your love, patience and unrelenting support.

INTRODUCTION

The root of any problem lies in the heart of the matter. Addressing symptoms or any concern, without a focus on the root cause, inevitably increases the chance of the problem resurfacing, with the risk of more complications.

The mind is the heart that fuels our behaviours, interactions, feelings and ultimately, the quality of our wellbeing in every way. The role of the physical heart is often easier appreciated as the engine that runs our bodies. The mind is no less important, hence the saying, "no health without mental health". Minding the mind is therefore essential for mental health.

It is said "no one can do your push ups for you". Whatever help there may be for mental health, every individual still has a role to play in tending the garden of their minds. Personal responsibility is a vital key to prevent the garden of the mind being taken over by undesirable plants and pests.

It is important to note that there are times help will be needed from others, especially when the burden of living becomes overwhelming. There are times when this engine, like the physical heart, needs specialist help, and not just maintenance or regular checks. It is therefore encouraged to reach out for appropriate help when the load of living becomes difficult to bear alone. Equally important is the need to reach out and help others, for no one is exempt from life storms. Together we are stronger.

The benefits of this book will not be optimized by reading through once. It is therefore recommended to be read repeatedly, and the exercises practiced regularly, as you would to benefit from physical exercise. Different mind muscles will be strengthened each time you re-read. *Blank pages have been left for reflections and to encourage starting new pages in thinking.*

Staying mentally fit and helping others to do the same, requires knowing how to care appropriately for the mind. Charity begins at home, so let us start with each person focusing on "minding my mind" and sharing keeping c-a-l-m with others.

KEEP C-A-L-M

You may not see it, but it is real. Pain, excitement, joy, disappointment, despair, are some of the feelings that affect the course of our lives.

Our thoughts and related feelings feed our choices in different ways, including relationships, career paths, and ultimately how fulfilling your life may or may not be. Learning to take charge of your thinking processes will undoubtedly change every aspect of your life.

Mind your mind.

Catch the thought

Address the thought

Lead the thought

Make a plan

You may never know why people behave the way they do ...

You can choose your response and how it affects you.

MINDING MY MIND

CATCH THE THOUGHT

Your feelings are signals to alert you of a need to respond. That is, decide to embrace a good opportunity or address an imminent threat or danger. Feelings are triggered by perception, including smell, taste, memories or information, and these rousing a thought like "something is wrong", "they are trying to cheat me", "this is an exceptionally good opportunity". An appropriate response is then required, with one thought rapidly triggering another with a risk of starting a wildfire.

You perceive feelings that are uncomfortable, distressing or terrifying. Feelings have roots and may stem from a past painful experience or knowledge, with the memory triggering an alarm. Feelings may also be roused by unfamiliarity, with the familiar zone usually being more comfortable, even if unhealthy at times. Identifying the roots of your feelings, will help in dealing with the specific cause of the distressing emotion.

Thinking is invisible work.

The stem may be a phrase, that keeps repeating itself, like "I am in trouble", pestering the mind and stirring fear. Emotional guards have been roused as there is something unusual, and phrases are beeping so you may respond. Unusual or unfamiliar, may however not be a threat, and it could be an opportunity. The roots of the feeling may be from the seeds of an event long forgotten. Check the trail and catch the thought and when the seeds were sown. Is the thought beneficial or detrimental? The thought may have started with a trigger from a forgotten comment by a friend or parent, incubated in the heart, now sprouting thorns of hurtful thoughts.

Identifying thoughts like "I am a failure", may lead to the next step: "why do I think I am a failure?" It may relate to an event tucked away in memory cells. Catching this thought is the primary step in facing the mind's bully, rather than letting the harmful seeds grow. It can be more terrifying facing some bullies than others, so help may be needed in addressing these issues. Unidentified, a toxic thought begins a process of contaminating healthy processes and systems. Professional help may be required when the thought has caused extensive damage, or the thought is proving too difficult to catch. Catching the thought, like identifying the specific virus causing undesirable symptoms of illness is a vital step in mind minding.

Check: What is the predominant thought that is fueling this desirable/undesirable feeling?

Taking your thoughts captive means controlling them instead of letting them control you

ADDRESS THE THOUGHT

Feelings need to be labelled. Is the thought fueling this feeling helpful or dreadful? Allowing unhealthy thoughts to stay is like deliberately harming yourself. Therefore, address the thought so you can post it where it belongs, trash can or treasure chest. The trash can of being easily available, like memory banks, leaves a risk of going fishing.

Labelling the thought correctly helps to disempower the intimidation of uncertainty and enhances clarity in dealing with the situation. Labelling challenging thoughts for what they are, helps in identifying the appropriate intervention required.

It is important not to deny the feeling. It is ok to say, "I feel scared", when dreading an outcome to be unfavorable. Acknowledge the fear and anxious feelings, then focus on what you would prefer to happen or accomplish. Take charge by telling yourself, "I feel scared", "this feeling will not stop me from achieving my goal". Positive affirmations help, noting what we hear often enough is taken into the mind. Affirming "I am in charge of my thought processing" and "I will keep moving towards my dreams". Reminders like, "this challenge is for a season" have also been known to help, noting the season will pass, like in times past and indeed like seasons of life.

This is not denying an issue that may need addressing, like a relationship difficulty or financial problem, but recognizing and dealing with detrimental thoughts. Using bleach as water would be harmful and could be fatal! It is important to address any thought for what it truly is, to harness the benefit or avert danger.

Give the thought its label – address it.

You may be offered a great opportunity or be considering taking a new role. Feelings of self-doubt may be overwhelming. Label it truthfully, "self-doubt" and re-affirm "this is an opportunity for growth", "I will step forward in spite of self-doubt". Naming the thought for what it is, helps towards dealing with it appropriately, including confronting the threat it poses. It's not enough to recognize a malignancy, it is important to identify the type.

Check: Am I being truthful about my feelings?

MINDING MY MIND

LEAD THE THOUGHT

If you are overwhelmed by negative feelings, you may have allowed unhealthy thoughts to slip into the driving seat of your mind, like fearful or unduly anxious thoughts. Please remember, you are the one in charge. Difficult feelings are not an indication to let go of the wheel and rather a signal to take a firmer grip and focus on the road.

You may already have jumped out of the driving seat and given up on a task or your dreams. Yes, there are times one needs a rest to recharge the mind batteries. You can get back in the driving seat, restart the engine and continue driving to your goals and dreams. **Take charge**, it is a thought that threatened your focus, and you can reframe it to serve you better.

Lead the thought before it leads you to unpleasant realms and becomes overwhelming. Thoughts need to be tamed by leading them, else there is a risk of unruliness and chaos. Lead the thought out of the driving seat of your mind if it is unhealthy or unhelpful. You have caught it and addressed it and it now must be led, taken charge of, to keep the mind healthy.

Helpful thoughts should be nurtured to empower the mind, like good seeds for a desired garden. Healthy thoughts make good company and give light on the road, while you stay in the driving seat of life. Unhelpful thoughts may persist irritatingly like stubborn weed needing more than the casual gardener's strength. Extra help may be required to deal with some very harmful thoughts, like talking to an insightful friend or getting professional help.

Lead the thought before it leads you where you do not desire.

Leading the thought involves action, like turning on the light for the dark thoughts to retreat. Writing crystallizes thinking, so write down the healthier thought and focus on that. Replace thoughts like "I am doomed", "I am a failure" with "I need help to deal with this", "I will acquire the skills to do this work" then start planning in line with the healthier thought. You could also keep declaring your helpful affirmation or get help to turn on the light. Affirmations help reprogram your brain and detoxify the mind. Repeating "my past is not a determinant of my future" with conviction will gradually help in embracing thoughts of a defined desired future and disengage from self-sabotaging thoughts from past experiences.

Check: Am I putting in the effort to keep my mind healthy? Am I taking the lead in minding my mind?

A man is what he thinks about all day long -

Ralph Waldo Emerson

MAKE A PLAN

Setting out on a journey is best done with a destination in mind, else you could easily end up anywhere which could be dangerous. Defining a plan makes it easier to stay on track. If your desire of having healthy thoughts and feelings is defined, it would be easier to spot anything contrary and address it. You may not be able to stop people knocking on your door, but you can put in devices to identify callers and choose which knocks to answer. What devices or strategies do you have in place to filter what thoughts are to be nurtured or rejected? Undefined focus subjects the mind easily to unhealthy distractions.

A bad experience is bound to repeat itself, if a better plan to manage it is not made. You may have handled past situations by throwing a tantrum and reacting instead of responding healthily. The future can be better with a plan in place for thought management. Your reactions and responses start with thought management.

*Have a **MAP** – **Make A Plan***

What is healthy for my mind? Think back on healthy strategies that have been helpful and make a list. The listed strategies will be weapons in your mental arsenal to combat negative thoughts. Listening to healthy music, talking to a friend, exercise, praying or journaling are some activities that help when the mind is challenged with unhelpful thoughts.

Regularly exercising strategies to accommodate healthy thoughts and ward off toxic thoughts, will strengthen your mind's muscles in building immunity and resilience for future threats. If this happens again, what will I do? So, keep practicing, to develop healthier reflex responses, for when your calm or healthy mind state is challenged. A defined plan helps to focus and guide from a current to a healthier mind state.

You cannot keep birds from flying over your head, but you can keep them from building a nest in your hair – Martin Luther

Check: What is my plan to mind my mind? Is my focus for my mind health defined?

MAKE A PLAN

MIND CARE

Mind care is ensuring appropriate and specific measures are in place for promoting mental health. This therefore includes feeding the mind, ensuring boundaries for protection, and leaving margins for the mind to develop. The boundaries are to protect from emotional pests and thieves. The boundaries should not be so restraining that there is no freedom to grow. Restrictions that hinder mind development, are detrimental to the individual involved and to others who lose benefits of the person's gifts and talents.

The mind like a puppy, must be tamed, else may bring shame or make life lame ~ 'Wonuola Akintola

---

Remember you are unique. You have no duplicate, for no two people are the same. Your unique gifts and talents need a healthy, appropriate environment and room for you to flourish. What makes one person grow may be toxic to another person, so know your mind to empower as well as shield it. Take note of the things that rouse wells of joy within, and let these strengthen you, while you keep exercising strategies to keep calm and focus on being a healthier you.

Care needs to be ensured that the mind is not so guarded that desired development is compromised.

You do not want to be so careful with people to the point of avoiding healthy interactions that would be of benefit to your mental wellbeing or impair your health in any way. Margins for promoting mind health are as important as boundaries for guarding the mind. Be careful about who and what gets into your mind but leave room to stretch and grow towards healthy goals.

Set your boundaries but leave margins for growth.

Check: What boundaries and margins do I need to set to protect my mind?

NEEDS, SEEDS AND WEEDS

What feelings do you desire?

Your response to this question may be feelings of happiness, love, joy, peace, contentment, fulfillment or feeling accepted.

There are times you may however crave negative feelings, like longing to be angry at perceived injustice, wishing to be unduly assertive to address feeling cheated. Feelings of being looked down on may rouse a desire for feeling powerful. Desired feelings without healthy reasons are bound to cause harm.

Everything starts with a thought.

Perceived injustice, ingratitude from others or abuse, may stir angry and revengeful thoughts. Your consequent unhappy or angry feeling may however not address the ill treatment appropriately, except the fueling though is healthily led. Are the thoughts making you feel the way you do, helpful or unhelpful? Will nurturing this thought do you good in any way? Should you be feeling angry rather than a feeling of indifference?

What you believe is what you live.

Is there a better way to address a matter without hosting a distressing thought for too long? Remember the body feels the impact of our thoughts, positive and negative. How long should a distressing thought be hosted for? Angry thoughts, for example, may help in taking steps to put things right, but kept in for longer than needed becomes a strain on the mind with symptoms like headache and lack of sleep.

A healthy response may be reporting to the appropriate authority, behaviours that puts you or others at risk, rather than letting anger stew and fuel an unhealthy reaction. The earlier the appropriate steps are initiated in addressing the perceived ill, the earlier your mind is unburdened, and your physical health protected or improved.

Every need has a seed.

NEEDS

What are your needs? A healthier mind or a stress filled mind?
Your needs should determine the seeds you invest in. Every activity, interaction, relationship, bears fruit over time. The fruits and harvest may be in the short, medium or long term but a yield is certain if the seed is preserved and nurtured. Let your needs determine your seeds, so choose your activities, relationships and time investment with care.

SEEDS

What kind of situations make you happy, motivated to do good or feel fulfilled? What energizes you to engage in healthy activities, like helping others in attaining healthy goals? These situations or activities may be seen like healthy seeds for your mind that make living rewarding and purposeful. Feeding your mind with nutritious information, regular exercise and healthy social interaction and relaxation, are some of the activities that re-energizes mind batteries. It is important to know what works for you.

> *Know your **needs** to sow your **seeds**,*
> *else easily you may feed the weeds!*
>
> - *'Wonuola Akintola*

WEEDS

There are also things that may threaten to drain the mind of energy and will if allowed! The activities and relationships that may subject you to undue pressure or abuse, feelings of helplessness, worthlessness, feeling devalued or losing motivation to engage in meaningful activities, may be seen as weeds.

These unhealthy situations, words or associations may have resulted in you acting regretfully. How have you addressed such scenarios in the past? What is a better and healthier way for you to deal with such issues? Preparation is key for any endeavor to be successful. The seeds may not look like the fruits they bear, so it is important to know your seeds, so you can choose the fruits you desire to harvest.

MY PLAN

What thought am I dwelling on now? (if unhealthy, consider the healthier thought and write it)

If unhealthy, what thought would be a healthier thought to address the same issue?

If the thought is healthy, what activities have helped in sustaining this thought?

MY PLAN

What seeds (healthy or unhealthy) am I sowing now with the thought I am focusing on?

What unhealthy thought do I need to address / label and take charge of / lead?

What would be a healthier thought to reframe the situation?

Keep **CALM***!*

The happiness of your life depends on the quality of
your thoughts ~ Marcus Aurelius

MY PLAN

What thought(s) have I allowed my mind to host, to my benefit or to my detriment?

What boundaries do I need to ensure to guard my mind and the thoughts that come?

What healthy margins do I need to ensure with boundaries and room for my mind's healthy development?

FOCUS AND FEELINGS

The mind is reported to think between 50,000 – 80,000 thoughts per day, suggesting at least 2,000 thoughts per hour. Most of these thoughts are noted to be purposeless, like comments the mind makes about self or others, questions like wondering what would happen if the cat drove the car. Every thought uses energy.

Processing the thoughts requires energy, the availability of which is limited. Choosing what thought to process is therefore important, as part of measures to determine your mood and consequent behaviour. Thoughts of rejection or failure, if not directed positively, would easily result in depressive feelings. The thought you focus on fuels your feelings.

Yes, there are many thoughts scurrying by, some enticing your attention more than others. It takes effort to select which thought deserves your focus. *The negative thoughts may be more demanding than the healthy thoughts, like news headlines.* **The positive thoughts may be less aggressive like treasure mines, requiring energy and skill to mine.**

Every skill gets better with use.

Focus is more than a glance, more intense than a gaze and births results of feelings, which may be positive or negative, determined by the object of focus.

Focusing is a skill that requires energy and involves sustained effort. **Persistence** is therefore required as you exercise choice with focusing.

Choosing your focus, in choosing healthy thoughts, is energy well invested and the returns increase with practice.

Check:
What are you focused on now?
Is your thought beneficial or detrimental to you?
What thought would be healthier for you to focus on?

FOCUS AND FEELINGS

What thought am I focusing on?
It is time to catch the thought.

What feeling/emotion is it rousing? Healthy or unhealthy?

What thought should I focus on, healthy or unhealthy?
Who determines the thought I focus on?

MY PLAN

Who is in the driving seat of my life? What thought keeps the current driver in the seat?

Who should be in the driving seat of my life?

What thought(s) do I need to nurture for my life to go in a healthier direction?

It always starts with a thought.
What you see, what you feel,
Started unseen, with a thought,
and birthed that called "reality."

IF CHANGE MUST BE,
IT NEEDS A NEW THOUGHT
TO START

YOUR MIND MATTERS

Uncertainty is certain,
Like life's oft unpredictable seasons.
Your mind, the central processing unit,
Deals with suggestions, ideas and thoughts,
For better or for worse.

Minding your mind is,
Minding the course of your life,
Guarding what thoughts are fuelled or starved,
For once in, it is your freedom to choose,
The direction the thoughts take you.

Your life matters,
Hence your mind matters,
Please guard your mind attentively,
For minding your mind is
Minding your life.

~ Wonuola Akintola

Minding your mind is minding your life.

THE HEART, THE MIND

The heart is a vital organ for physical health, the same applies to the mind for emotional wellbeing in every area of life. A healthy heart can take on activities of daily life without physical distress of undue discomfort. A healthy mind enjoys daily activities, including work, relationships, social interactions and helps others do the same.

The need for minding the mind cannot be over emphasized, and as the saying goes there is "no health without mental health". The fuel for joyful and meaningful living is generated from a healthy mind with healthy thoughts, keeping us not just alive but living healthy.

Keep your mind healthy to fuel you in fulfilling your unique purpose in living for mind health is life wealth.
Enjoy the freedom in minding your mind.

Best Wishes,

'Wonuola Akintola
https://www.wonuola.com

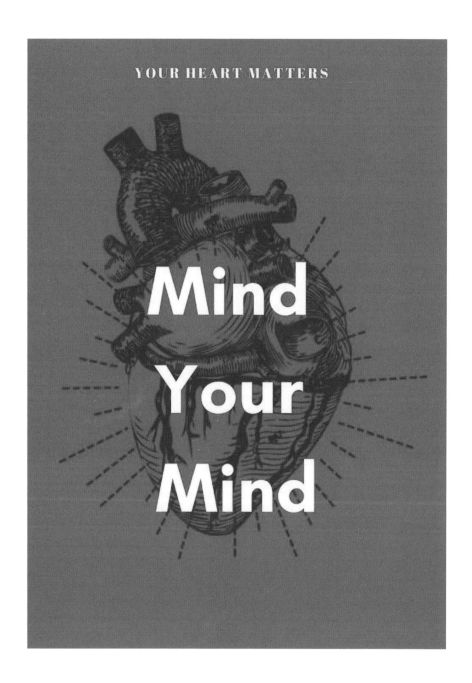

ABOUT THE AUTHOR

'Wonuola Akintola is an Independent Mind Health Consultant and Founding Director of FountWealth Consultancy and Training Services.

Following her graduation from the College of Medicine, University of Ibadan, Nigeria, 'Wonuola trained in Paediatric medicine and surgery in the United Kingdom. She subsequently specialized in Child and Adolescent Psychiatry. 'Wonuola works part time as a locum consultant in the Children and Adolescent Mental Health Service, with the National Health Service, developing her interest in neuro-developmental disorders.

A certified Speaker, Trainer and Coach with the John Maxwell team, as well as being a certified Family and Parenting Coach, 'Wonuola extends her services globally, speaking, coaching and training on mind health in various settings and facilitating programs for youth and families.

'Wonuola's passion for holistic health, focuses her writing, speaking and training on mind empowerment for enriching lives, with a conviction that health is wealth, and mental health the foundation for holistic health.

Printed in Great Britain
by Amazon